FRANKLIN & ELEANOR
ROOSEVELT

PRESIDENTS
and
FIRST LADIES

iBooks
Habent Sua Fata Libelli

Ruth Ashby

Please visit our web site at:
www.ibooksforyoungreaders.com
Manhanset House
POB 342
Dering Harbor, New York 11965

Library of Congress Cataloging-in-Publication Data
Ashby, Ruth.
    Franklin & Eleanor Roosevelt / by Ruth Ashby.
    p. cm — (Presidents and first ladies)
    Includes bibliographical references and index.

  1. Roosevelt, Franklin D. (Franklin Delano), 1882-1945—Juvenile literature. 2. Roosevelt, Eleanor, 1884-1962—Juvenile literature. 3. Presidents—United States—Biography—Juvenile literature. 4. Presidents' spouses—United States—Biography—Juvenile literature. 5. Married people—United States— Biography—Juvenile literature. I. Tide: Franklin and Eleanor Roosevelt. II. Tide.

E807.A87 2005   973.917'092—dc22   [B]   2004057738

ISBN: 978-1-59687-656-9

Copyright © 2005 by Byron Preiss Visual Publications
Produced by Byron Preiss Visual Publications Inc.
Project Editor: Kelly Smith
Photo Researcher: Bill White

Photo Credits: AP/Wide World: 4 (top), 8,16 (top), 21 (bottom), 23,28, 34; CORBIS: 16 (bottom), 26 (top); Courtesy of the Franklin D. Roosevelt Digital Archives: 5, 6 (top and bottom), 7, 9,10,11,12,13,14,19, 20, 21 (top), 22,24,25,27, 30, 32, 33, 35, 36, 37, 38, 39,41,42; Library of Congress: 4 (bottom), 26 (bottom)
Cover art: AP/Wide World

August 2024

CONTENTS

Words that appear in the glossary are printed in
boldface type the first time they occur in the text.

▶ INTRODUCTION ★★★★★★★★★★

On January 28, 1941, columnist Raymond Clapper listed Eleanor Roosevelt as one of the "Ten Most Powerful People in Washington" in an article for *Look* magazine. The wife of President Franklin D. Roosevelt, Clapper said, was "a force on public opinion, on the President and on the government . . . the most influential woman of our times." For nearly thirty-five years of political life, Franklin depended on Eleanor's inexhaustible energy and social conscience to inform him about critical issues affecting millions of U.S. citizens. Franklin and Eleanor Roosevelt developed a unique working partnership that would see them, and the country, through the Great Depression, the New Deal, and World War II.

Franklin Delano Roosevelt in 1933.

Together they accomplished great things. Their marriage was complicated by many factors, however, and over the years they were often apart, both physically and emotionally. Yet their mutual admiration and respect always remained. "I hated to see you go, . . ." Eleanor once wrote Franklin in early 1931 as he set off for Europe. "We are really very dependent on each other though we do see so little of each other. . . . Goodnight, dear. . . . I miss you & hate to feel you so far away."

Eleanor Roosevelt in 1933.

CHAPTER ONE

A PRIVILEGED UPBRINGING

When Franklin Delano Roosevelt was five years old, his father, James, took him to visit President Grover Cleveland. The story goes that Cleveland, worn out by the demands of the office, patted the boy's head and said, "My little man, I am making a strange wish for you. It is that you may never be President of the United States."

Certainly Franklin, who could trace his lineage back to Dutch settlers who came to the Hudson River Valley in upstate New York about 1640, was bred to succeed. Thrifty and industrious, the Roosevelts had made a fortune in real estate and trade, especially in West Indies sugar and rum. Franklin's father James served on the boards of several corporations, but he spent most of his time at Springwood, his sprawling country estate near the town of Hyde Park, New York. In 1880, after his first wife died, James married a society beauty, Sara Delano, twenty-six years younger than her husband.

Franklin and his mother in Washington, D.C., in 1887.

Franklin was born in an upstairs bedroom at Springwood on January 30, 1882. Recording the event in his diary that night, James wrote, "At quarter to nine my Sallie had a splendid large baby boy. He weighs 10 pounds [about 5 kilograms] without his clothes." The Roosevelts were adoring parents. Sarah hovered over her beloved only son, keeping a diary of everything he did and setting him a strict schedule of activities. James introduced him to horseback riding, swimming, and sledding. Growing up in the company of adults, young Franklin was especially poised and well spoken, a cheerful, attentive youngster with many interests and hobbies.

This 1893 photograph shows eleven-year-old Franklin in his riding outfit.

Educated at home by tutors, Franklin learned English grammar, history, science, math, literature, Latin, German, and French. "What he reads, he seems to remember with a memory that's like flypaper," his mother said admiringly. "Everything sticks to it."

An essential part of Franklin's education was derived from traveling to Europe with his parents—eight trips by the time he was fourteen—and spending summers on Campobello Island, off the coast of New Brunswick, Canada. He was an avid stamp collector as well as an eager sailor on his father's 51-foot (about 16-meter) yacht, the *Half Moon*. His fascination with the sea was inspired by his grandfather, Warren Delano, a sea captain who had made his fortune in trade in China. By age twelve, Franklin had discovered the books of American naval historian Alfred Thayer Mahan, an important advocate for a strong U.S. Navy.

A Gentleman's Education

In 1896, when Franklin turned fourteen, his reluctant parents sent him away to a boarding school in Groton, Massachusetts. "It is hard to leave our darling boy," his mother admitted. Short and slim when he arrived, Franklin was not a natural athlete, and he started out on the worst baseball and football teams in the school. Even after he shot up to about 6 feet (183 centimeters), he never advanced any higher than the second-best football team. Yet he was a good student who graduated in the top fourth of his class and won the Latin prize, a forty-volume set of Shakespeare. Years later, after Franklin had become famous, Groton's headmaster, the Reverend Endicott Peabody, said that his star graduate was "a quiet, satisfactory boy of more than ordinary intelligence, . . . but not brilliant. . . . We all liked him."

Franklin (top row, center) with the Groton baseball team. He was team manager in 1899.

Peabody urged his privileged young charges to enter public service, like Franklin's famous fifth cousin, Theodore Roosevelt, then secretary of the Navy. In 1898, Cousin Teddy became a national hero when he led his volunteer cavalry, the Rough Riders, up San Juan Hill in Cuba and helped secure a U.S. victory in the **Spanish-American War**. Franklin took Peabody's advice to heart. Years later, he would say that his headmaster's influence meant "more . . . than that of any other people next to my father and mother."

After Groton, Franklin attended Harvard College, class of 1903. During his freshman year, his father died of the heart condition that had long ailed him. His distraught mother immediately rented an apartment in Boston to be near her son.

Franklin (top row, center) poses in a Harvard class of 1904 group shot at Nantasket Beach, Massachusetts.

Franklin's most notable accomplishment at Harvard was to join the daily newspaper, the *Crimson*. He got his first scoop when Cousin Teddy, then vice president of the United States, told him in confidence that he would be addressing a class in constitutional government the next day. Franklin leaked the story, hundreds of students showed up for the lecture, and Franklin was promoted to editor. By the time he graduated, he would rise to become editor-in-chief.

Franklin also experienced failure, however, when he was turned down by the Porcellian, the most exclusive social club at Harvard. He never discovered why, but he later said that the rejection was his "greatest disappointment in life."

There was plenty else to keep him busy and Franklin enjoyed the Hasty Pudding Theatricals, the Fly Club, the rowing club, and other activities. Yet despite all the dinners and dances he regularly attended, he had no steady female companionship. All that changed in 1903 when he fell in love.

Theodore Roosevelt

In the mid 1700s, five generations before Franklin was born, Jacobus Roosevelt founded a line of Roosevelts who settled along the Hudson River. His brother Johannes stayed in the city, and his grandchildren and great-grandchildren summered on Long Island. Eventually, Jacobus's descendants—Franklin among them—became known as the Hyde Park Roosevelts. Johannes's descendants were the Oyster Bay Roosevelts, and their most famous member was Theodore Roosevelt.

Born in New York City in 1858, Theodore was badly asthmatic as a boy and had to work hard to build up his strength. As an adult, he was known for his boundless and indomitable energy. Theodore Roosevelt was a scholar, writer, soldier, rancher, conservationist, and big-game hunter. At age twenty-three, he became a New York State assemblyman, at thirty-seven, head of the New York City Police Department, and at thirty-nine, the assistant secretary of the Navy. At forty, he continued his career as governor of New York, and two years later became vice president of the United States. Six months after his inauguration, on September 14, 1901, Theodore Roosevelt became president of the United States when President William McKinley died from an assassin's bullet. Roosevelt was the youngest man ever to hold that office.

As president, Roosevelt put many progressive reforms into practice. He broke up illegal business **monopolies**; passed laws regulating the railroad, meat-packing, and food industries; and set up a national nature conservation program. Far from being an **isolationist**, he worked to position the United States as an international power by strengthening the Navy. Under Roosevelt's direction, workers began to dig a canal that would provide a shorter trade route between the Atlantic and Pacific Oceans through the narrow Central American country of Panama. Today, historians consider Theodore Roosevelt to be one of the strongest presidents in U.S. history.

Theodore Roosevelt (center) poses with members of the Rough Riders in this 1898 photo.

A DIFFICULT CHILDHOOD

The childhood of Anna Eleanor Roosevelt was as different as possible from that of the man she would someday marry. Whereas Franklin was adored by his overprotective parents, Eleanor was ignored, deserted, and finally, left an orphan.

Eleanor was born in New York City on October 11, 1884, to a beautiful socialite, Anna Hall Roosevelt, and her good-looking, charming husband, Elliot Roosevelt. The little girl was so painfully shy and solemn that her mother called her Granny. Dismayed by her plain daughter, who had a bad overbite and a receding chin, Anna Hall Roosevelt once told her, "You have no looks, so see to it that you have manners." All of her life, Eleanor would be self-conscious about her supposed lack of beauty.

Eleanor and her father Elliott in New York City on April 30, 1899.

Elliot Roosevelt, Theodore Roosevelt's younger brother, made up for his wife's coldness by being affectionate and loving. "He was the one great love of my life as a child," Eleanor later confessed. "I never doubted that I stood first in his heart." However, Elliot was a troubled man who suffered from alcoholism as well as depression and frequently cheated on Anna. By the time Eleanor was seven, he had been banished from his wife and children by his disapproving older brother, who had taken over the family finances. Not until Elliot rehabilitated himself, Theodore Roosevelt decreed, could he return.

Tragedies followed in quick succession. The next year, Eleanor's twenty-nine-year-old mother died from **diphtheria,** and Eleanor and her younger brothers, Elliot Jr. and Hall, were sent to live in Grandmother Hall's great gloomy house in Tivoli, New York. Eleanor kept up a correspondence with her absent father. She remembers his instruction "to be a good girl, not to give any trouble, to study hard, [and] to grow up into a woman [I] could be proud of." She treasured the brief time she spent with him on his infrequent visits, but no matter how much he loved his children, Elliot could not reform himself. Once, in New York City, when he and Eleanor were out together walking his fox terriers, he left her waiting on the sidewalk for six hours after he went into the Knickerbocker Club for a drink. Finally, the doorman took the patient little girl home.

In the spring of 1894, Eleanor's little brother, Elliot, also died of diphtheria. Then, when she was ten, her drunken father had a fall, lapsed into a coma, and died. To help cope with her grief, Eleanor retreated to a dream world in which she was the heroine and her father the hero. "From that time on," she remembered, "I lived with him more closely, probably, than I had when he was alive."

The ugly duckling grew tall and skinny, dressed in old-fashioned black stockings and high button boots. She was a conscientious student and avid reader and very insecure. "I was not only timid, I was afraid," Eleanor remembered, "afraid of almost everything, I think: of mice, of the dark, of imaginary dangers."

Becoming a Swan

Her mother had always wanted Eleanor to be educated abroad, so when Eleanor was fifteen, Grandmother Hall sent her to Allenswood, a boarding school outside London. Allenswood was Eleanor's salvation. The school's headmistress, Marie Souvestre,

Students at Eleanor's boarding school, Allenwood, gather in a courtyard, 1900. Here, Eleanor shed much of the insecurity that plagued her in her early years.

was a vibrant, forward-thinking French woman who encouraged her students to think critically about politics, society, and religion. She immediately recognized Eleanor's intelligence and sensitivity and took her under her wing. Under this perceptive tutelage, Eleanor blossomed into a graceful and self-assured young lady. Her three years at Allenswood, Eleanor wrote, were the "the happiest years of my life."

In turn, Marie Souvestre told Eleanor's grandmother that the girl had "the warmest heart I have ever encountered."

Eleanor had wanted to stay for her fourth year but was obliged to come back to New York at age eighteen for her formal debut into society. That winter, her life was dedicated to giving and receiving social calls and going to parties.

Eleanor did not want to devote her life merely to pleasure, however. Her years with Marie Souvestre had interested her in the plight of the poor and needy. Membership in a club for socially prominent young ladies called the Junior League gave her the opportunity to do volunteer work in the New York slums. She taught exercise and dancing to children in Rivington House, a housing development offering community services on the Lower East Side. For the Consumers' League, she visited **sweatshops** and **tenements** where immigrant women and children worked twelve-to fourteen-hour days. "I was appalled," Eleanor wrote later. "But this is what had been required of me and I wanted to be useful."

One afternoon, a young man she was dating came to pick her up at Rivington House and helped her escort home a little girl who had fallen ill. "He was absolutely shaken when he saw the cold-water tenement where the child lived," Eleanor remembered later, "and kept saying he simply could not believe human beings lived that way."

The young man was her fifth cousin, twenty-one-year-old Franklin Roosevelt.

Eleanor is eighteen in this photo, which was taken in honor of her debut into society, 1902.

KEEPING THE NAME IN THE FAMILY

s members of the large and active Roosevelt clan, Eleanor and Franklin had known each other since they were children. At a Christmas party in 1898 at her aunt's house, sixteen-year-old Franklin had gallantly asked the shy fourteen-year-old Eleanor to dance. When she returned from Europe, Eleanor ran into her attractive cousin again on a train from New York City, and they started to see each other socially. What began as friendship soon turned into romance.

Eleanor discovered a sympathetic, intelligent young man who read poetry with her. Still somewhat reserved herself, she opened up in the warmth of his charm and kindness. He was so handsome and socially at ease that at first she found it difficult to believe he could actually be interested in her. Franklin, however, had told his mother years before that "Cousin Eleanor has a very good mind." When she suddenly reappeared after years abroad, he discovered that she had luminous blue eyes, long, lovely, golden-brown hair, and a brilliant smile as well. He sensed in Eleanor a strength and steadiness of purpose that would help him achieve his goals.

One fall afternoon in 1903, after a Yale-Harvard football game, Franklin asked Eleanor to marry him, and she accepted. "After lunch I have a never to be forgotten walk to the river with my darling," he wrote in his diary.

"Everything is changed for me now," Eleanor wrote Franklin a few weeks later. "I am so happy. Oh! So happy & I love you *so* dearly."

Franklin and Eleanor in a relative's wedding party on June 18, 1904. They were secretly engaged at the time.

It took some effort to convince Franklin's jealous mother that they were serious. The couple were so young, Sara Roosevelt insisted, that they must keep the engagement a secret and wait a year before they married. Eleanor tried to win her future mother-in-law over. "I do want you to love me a little," she wrote the imposing matriarch. "You must know that I will always try to do as you wish." Reluctantly, Sara finally accustomed herself to the idea, and the wedding date was set.

On March 17, 1905—St. Patrick's Day—Franklin and Eleanor were married. Eleanor, looking beautiful in satin and lace, was given away by her uncle, Theodore Roosevelt, who was then the twenty-sixth president of the United States. Afterward, President Roosevelt turned to the groom and said, "Well, Franklin, there's nothing like keeping the name in the family."

Early Married Life

After their honeymoon, the newlyweds settled in New York City, where Franklin was studying for his law degree at Columbia University. Within three years, Sara Roosevelt bought adjoining town houses, separated by sliding doors, for herself and the new couple. Sara, not Eleanor, hired the servants, bought the furniture, and gave orders to the nursemaids. Eleanor was so young and eager to please that she was not mistress of her own home.

A portrait of Eleanor and Franklin with Anna and baby James in Hyde Park, New York in 1908.

Most of her energy, in any event, was taken up with childbearing. Over the next eleven years, she had six children: Anna Eleanor, 1906; James, 1907; Franklin Jr., 1909; Elliot, 1910; a second Franklin Jr., 1914; and John, 1916. The first Franklin Jr., died of influenza when he was only seven months old, and Eleanor was devastated. "I felt he had been left too much to the nurse . . . and that in some way I must be to blame," she wrote later.

Eleanor was a well-meaning but unprepared mother. Because she had grown up without adequate parenting herself, she barely knew how to relate to her own children when they were young. "It did not come naturally to me to understand little children or to enjoy them," she said. "Playing with children was difficult for me because play had not been an important part of my own childhood." Because Sara spoiled her grandchildren and Franklin was busy with his career, it usually fell to Eleanor to provide the discipline. Later she remarked that she had disciplined them too much.

Franklin, meanwhile, had embarked on a conventional New York law career, joining a Wall Street firm after graduating from law school. Soon, though, he was restless. Always before him shone the illustrious example of Cousin Teddy, president by age forty-two. Franklin Roosevelt longed to get into politics and follow in his cousin's footsteps.

The Roosevelt family in Washington, D.C., on June 12, 1919. From left to right: Anna, Franklin Jr., Franklin, Elliott, Eleanor, James, Sara, and John.

Choosing Politics

In 1910, Roosevelt made his first move when a group of Hyde Park Democrats asked him to run for the New York State Senate. He rented a bright-red roadster and drove it over the country roads of his native Dutchess County, stopping to address voters along the way. At first, he was an awkward speaker with a high-pitched voice and a habit of peering down his nose at people through his pince-nez, a type of eyeglasses. Soon, though, he had found his rhythm. Beginning every speech with a cheery, "My friends," he promised farmers he would fight for them.

Roosevelt won an upset victory in the heavily Republican district, and the family moved to Albany. There, while Eleanor hosted the social teas and dinners expected of a politician's wife, Franklin tried to make a name for himself. His battle against the deep-rooted and powerful influences of the Democratic organization called **Tammany Hall** made national headlines, and soon Franklin was regarded as one of the rising stars within his own party. He worried about his future, though, when he fell ill with **typhoid fever** just before the 1912 election. His solution was to hire a short, feisty newspaperman and political genius named Louis Howe. While the candidate was in bed recovering, Howe ran an advertising blitz that helped Roosevelt secure a victory.

In that year's presidential election, Franklin backed Democratic candidate Woodrow Wilson against Teddy Roosevelt. The two Roosevelts had long-standing loyalties to opposing parties despite their family ties. Teddy had split from the Republican Party to run an idealistic but impractical candidacy as the nominee from the newly formed Bull Moose Party. The introduction of this third party to the standard two-party contest divided the Republicans, and Wilson was elected. He promptly tapped Franklin to join the new administration as assistant secretary of the Navy. Franklin was only thirty-one years old.

Seated proudly at Teddy Roosevelt's old desk, Franklin plunged into his new job. Together with his boss, Josephus Daniels, Franklin urged Congress and the president to build up the nation's Navy when Europe entered into World War I in 1914. Already, German submarines, called U-boats, were threatening U.S. ships in the Atlantic Ocean. If the United States was to protect itself against Germany, it needed battleships and submarines. At a time when most U.S. citizens were isolationists, believing that the country should focus on national interests and avoid foreign intervention, Franklin Roosevelt urged President Wilson to take the initiative against Germany. For three years, Wilson avoided war, continuing to press the European powers for peace through negotiation. Not until March 1917, when the sinking of several U.S. ships by German submarines forced his hand, did Wilson ask Congress for a

As assistant secretary of the navy, Franklin practices shooting on the Marine Corps Rifle Range at Winthrop, Maryland, in 1917.

declaration of war. "The world must be made safe for democracy," he told the country.

The nation mobilized for war. As Franklin readied the Navy for action, Eleanor visited military hospitals and volunteered at a Red Cross canteen, serving soup and sandwiches to traveling servicemen. It was her first job outside of the home, and she was energized by the work. "I was learning to have a certain confidence in myself and in my ability to meet emergencies and deal with them," she remembered later.

A Shocking Discovery

During the summer of 1918, while Eleanor stayed in Washington, her husband sailed to Europe to inspect naval bases at the war front. Two months later, Franklin was sent home with double pneumonia. Unpacking his suitcases, Eleanor discovered a packet of letters from her attractive young social secretary Lucy Mercer. They confirmed what she had already feared: Her husband was having an affair. "The bottom dropped out of my own particular world," she

Lucy Mercer was Eleanor's social secretary. In 1918 Eleanor discovered Lucy's love letters to Franklin.

wrote later. "I faced myself and my world honestly for the first time." Devastated, she went into Franklin's sickroom and offered him a divorce.

In 1918, divorce was considered scandalous. It would ruin Roosevelt's reputation, his mother argued, begging Franklin to think of his children and his future. She even warned him that if he divorced Eleanor and married Lucy, she would cut him off without a penny. Roosevelt's political advisor, Louis Howe, was just as disturbed and told Roosevelt that divorce would destroy his political career. Howe tried to mediate between Franklin and Eleanor and convince them that it was better for them to stay together.

Finally, Franklin and Eleanor decided the marriage should continue. He would never see Lucy Mercer again, and they would go on, but their relationship would never be the same. Although they were still bound by love and respect, they had lost their emotional intimacy. From then on, Eleanor would carve out a separate sphere for herself, developing her own friends and interests. Still, together, Eleanor and Franklin would forge one of the most amazing political partnerships of the century.

In 1920, Roosevelt ran for vice president on the Democratic ticket with presidential nominee James M. Cox, governor of Ohio. Even though Cox lost to Republican Warren G. Harding, the campaign gave Roosevelt national exposure and experience. He was ready for the next big challenge.

World War I

On June 28, 1914, Austrian Archduke Franz Ferdinand and his wife Sophie were assassinated in Bosnia by a Serbian nationalist. Hostilities flared, and before long disputes over territory and money pitted the Central Powers (Germany, Austria-Hungary, and Turkey) against the Allied Powers (France, Great Britain, Russia, and twenty-one other nations). Between ten and twelve million soldiers died in the Great War, later known as World War I.

On the Western Front, the opponents faced off along a line of trenches that stretched across France and Belgium. Despite horrific battles costing hundreds of thousands of lives, neither side could win an advantage. In spring 1918, a year after the United States entered the war, American troops joined the front lines and broke the stalemate, pushing back the German army with the help of British and French forces. The war ended on November 11, 1918, known as Armistice Day. According to the harsh terms of the Versailles Treaty, Germany was forced to accept blame for the war and compensate the Allies for costly damages. Twenty years later, German determination to regain its former military might helped fuel World War II.

CHAPTER FOUR

THE CHALLENGE OF A LIFETIME

On the morning of August 11, 1921, Franklin Roosevelt awoke in his bedroom in his family's home on Campobello Island and attempted to swing his legs over the side of the bed. Just the day before, he had been sailing and swimming with his children and had gone to bed feeling tired and achy. Now, alarmingly, his left leg was so weak it collapsed when he tried to stand on it, and he had a fever. By afternoon, both legs were limp and he was in a great deal of pain.

Doctors diagnosed poliomyelitis, or polio, a virus that infects and paralyzes the muscles. Immediately, Eleanor became her husband's full-time caregiver. She bathed him, massaged his aching muscles, and tried to keep up his spirits. Franklin had moments of despair but tried to present a brave front, especially for the children, who were frightened to see their energetic father in the grip of a devastating illness.

Gradually it became apparent that Roosevelt would be disabled for a long time. Sara wanted her dear boy to come home to her estate at Hyde Park and take up the relaxed life of a country squire. If she had had her way, Franklin would have been treated as an invalid for the rest of his life. Eleanor and Louis Howe, however, fought to keep him independent, positive, and active. He still had a future in politics, they assured him, and they would help him achieve it. That winter, Eleanor fought with her mother-in-law for Franklin's future. She later called it "the most trying period of my life." Eleanor emerged from her battles stronger and more able, she said, to "stand on my own two feet in regard to my husband's life, my own life, and my children's training."

Franklin built up his torso, lifting weights and doing chin-ups on a bar above his bed. After his withered legs were fitted with heavy steel braces, he could walk with crutches or by leaning on someone else. He did not give up hope that he could walk unaided, however, and when in 1924 he heard about the healthful mineral springs at Warm Springs, Georgia, he went south to investigate. Soon he was delighted to discover that he could stand by himself in the soothing water. A few years later, he renovated the run-down resort, opening it to other members of the "Polio Gang," as he called the other guests. "Here is Dr. Roosevelt," he would announce when he rolled himself out to the pool in his wheel chair. "Now remember: You've got to know you're going to improve!"

Franklin Roosevelt never did regain the full use of his legs. His battle against polio strengthened his spirit, however. Of Roosevelt, his Secretary of Labor Frances Perkins later said, "The man emerged completely warm-hearted, with humility of spirit and with a deeper philosophy. Having been to the depths of trouble, he understood the problems of people in trouble."

Throughout it all, Roosevelt remained upbeat and optimistic. "If you have spent two years in bed trying to wiggle your big toe," he once said, "everything else seems easy."

Franklin Roosevelt in Warm Springs, Georgia in 1923. Franklin visited the springs as a treatment for polio, which damaged his leg muscles.

New Interests

Eleanor kept the Roosevelt name in the headlines during the years of Franklin's illness and recovery. She became interested in politics later than her husband did. When, years before, Franklin had originally come out in favor of women's **suffrage**, Eleanor hadn't known what to think. "I had never given the question serious thought," she admitted later, "for I took for granted that men were superior creatures and knew more about politics than women did." In the 1920s, the more mature and experienced Eleanor worked on the Democratic Party National Woman's Committee and on the Women's Trade Union League, an organization to secure better conditions for working women. She was coached in public speaking by Louis Howe, who advised her to get rid of her nervous giggle. "Have something to say, say it, and then sit," he told her bluntly.

The "Three Musketeers": Eleanor (left) with friends Marion Dickerman (center) and Nancy Cook (right) at Campobello in 1926.

She began to make new friends, including Nancy Cook, a political organizer who was also a carpenter and jewelry maker, and Cook's good friend Marion Dickerman, a teacher at the Todhunter School, a private girls' school in Manhattan. The three became nearly inseparable. At the suggestion of Franklin, who called them the "Three Musketeers," they decided to build a house together on the Roosevelt property at Hyde Park. Cook and Dickerman moved into Val-Kill cottage, as the house was called, while Eleanor often came to visit. Eleanor also began teaching history, government, and literature part time at Todhunter.

Political Comeback

Franklin was spending much of his time in Warm Springs, still trying to walk again, and commuting to New York City, where he had resumed a career in law. In 1924, he and Howe decided it was time for a political comeback. Roosevelt made his return by nominating New York governor Al Smith for president. At the National Democratic Convention in Madison Square Garden, New York City, Franklin was hoisted onto the stage out of sight of the audience. Holding tightly to his son Jimmy's arm and leaning on his cane, he walked to the podium, where he was greeted with tumultuous applause. Roosevelt was back.

Smith lost this nomination—but won the next, in 1928. He was prepared to give up the New York governor's office in order to run for president, but he wanted his friend Franklin to take his place as governor. Franklin was reluctant. He and Howe were both convinced that 1928 would be a banner year for the Republicans, who had nominated businessman Herbert Hoover for president. He didn't want to be swamped by a Hoover landslide. Smith made it clear that Roosevelt didn't have a choice—he had to run for the sake of the party.

Franklin campaigned for governor in a roadster with a metal bar across the back seat. At each stop, when he pulled himself up, his braces would lock into place and he would speak from a standing position. Roosevelt seemed so vital that voters forgot he was disabled. On election night, Republican Herbert Hoover won the presidency by a landslide, as predicted, even in New York State. Yet Roosevelt squeaked by to victory in the governor's race.

"Happy Days Are Here Again"

On January 1, 1929, Franklin Delano Roosevelt was inaugurated as governor of New York. Ten months later, the stock market tumbled, plunging the nation into the Great Depression. In New York as elsewhere, people lost their jobs, families lost their homes, and children went hungry. Franklin brought experts—economists, labor experts, professors—to Albany to address the dire situation. "Let's try everything and anything," Roosevelt told his "brain trust," as the group was called. "If one thing doesn't work, we'll try something else. Above all, try *something*!" He persuaded the state legislature to pass laws to raise income taxes on the wealthy, to create new jobs, and to provide temporary food and shelter. Citizens contrasted his **activism** with the **laissez-faire** attitude of President Herbert Hoover, who shortsightedly insisted that "prosperity is just around the corner."

Roosevelt won reelection by a landslide in 1930. Eleanor, who was in New York City on election night preparing to teach a class, sent him an admiring note: "*Much love & a world of congratulations. It is a triumph in so many ways, dear & so well earned. Bless you & good luck these next two years.—ER.*"

Franklin Roosevelt and Al Smith in Albany, New York, in 1930.

Franklin Roosevelt delivers his acceptance speech at the Democratic **National Convention** in Chicago on July 2, 1932.

The Great Depression

In the United States in the 1920s, it seemed that the good times would last forever. Employment was high, industry was booming, and people went on a spending spree. Those who did not have the cash to buy a new car or refrigerator could buy on an installment plan, paying just a bit each month. They bought stocks the same way, putting down ten percent and borrowing the rest. Soon everyone was playing the stock market, trying to "get rich quick." Stock prices soared, and by early 1929, economists worried that the boom would end soon.

On October 24, 1929, nervous investors started selling their stocks. Suddenly, there was a stampede of selling—but no one was buying. By the close of the day on October 29, called Black Tuesday, stocks were nearly worthless. The economy plunged downhill. As investors went bankrupt, businesses closed, workers were laid off, savings were wiped out, and banks were forced to close their doors. By 1932, one in four workers was unemployed, and millions were homeless. The United States was in the worst depression in its history.

A soup kitchen during the Great Depression.

Roosevelt's aggressive approach to his state's economic woes had made him the front-runner for the Democratic nomination for president in 1932. In long sessions with his "brain trust," Roosevelt wrestled with the problems of the country and began to develop solutions. He scorned Hoover's notion that prosperity would somehow "trickle down" from the most to the least prosperous element in society. The government, he declared in a radio address, must "build from the bottom up and not from the top down [and] put their faith once more in the forgotten man at the bottom of the economic pyramid."

In Albany, Franklin and Eleanor listened to a radio broadcast of his nomination for president, and then they flew together to the Democratic convention in Chicago. The band played Roosevelt's theme song, "Happy Days Are Here Again," as he went on stage. With his trademark grin, Roosevelt took command. "I pledge you, I pledge myself, to a new deal for the American people," he declared.

The nation took him at his word. Roosevelt captured the presidency from Hoover, winning forty-two out of fifty states. Franklin and Eleanor were going to the White House.

CHAPTER FIVE

A NEW PRESIDENCY AND A NEW DEAL

Roosevelt is sworn in as president on March 4, 1933. He can be seen in the middle of the photo, above the podium.

Franklin Roosevelt came to the presidency in a time of crisis. In the four months between November 1932, when he was elected, and March 1933, when he took office, the country slid further into depression. Without the funds needed to pay clients, the banking system was near collapse. As small banks failed, people lost their life savings. They hoped the nation's new president could help them.

As Franklin Delano Roosevelt was sworn in as president on the cold, blustery morning of March 4, 1933, citizens gathered around their radios, eager for some words of comfort and inspiration. "This great nation will endure as it has endured, will revive and will prosper," Roosevelt assured his listeners in rousing tones. "So, first of all, let me assert my firm belief that the only thing we have to fear is fear itself." He would take "action and action now," he promised.

The Hundred Days

In his first three months in office—known as the Hundred Days—Roosevelt kept his word, pushing a record-breaking number of laws through Congress to deal with the emergency. The economic recovery program that these laws and others created was called Roosevelt's New Deal.

First, two days after the inauguration, he called for a bank holiday. All the banks in the country were closed for eight days, while their economic health was assessed. During this time, Congress passed the Emergency Banking Relief Act, which decreed that all banks would be examined and only those with sufficient funds would be allowed to reopen. At the end of the holiday, Roosevelt delivered his first national radio broadcast to explain the measures he had taken to rescue the banking system and secure depositors' money. "It is safer to keep your money in a reopened bank than it is under the mattress," he assured his listeners. Reassured depositors returned their money to the banks.

FDR delivers one of his many "fireside chats" in Washington, D.C., on April 28, 1935.

This was just the first of thirty public addresses, called "fireside chats," which Roosevelt would give to communicate directly with the American people. As one newspaperman wrote, Roosevelt's "exuberant vitality . . . high spirits . . . tirelessness . . . gave a lift to the spirits of millions of average men, stimulated them to high use of their own power, gave them a new zest for life."

Other reforms followed quickly. The New Deal was based on the three *R*s: relief for the unemployed; recovery for the economy; and reform to prevent another depression. FDR, as Roosevelt was known, enacted an "alphabet soup" of new programs. There was the Civilian Conservation Corps (CCC), which paid unemployed young men—2.5 million men in all—to work in forests and parks. Men and women of the Works Project Administration (WPA) were hired to build roads, bridges, airports, and hospitals; paint murals and put on plays; record folk tunes and slave narratives. The Federal Emergency Relief Administration (FERA) gave money to state and local agencies, which in turn gave it to people in need. To pay for all the new programs, Roosevelt raised taxes on wealthy people and on corporations. He also spent more than he took in through taxes in an attempt to jumpstart economic growth.

Eleanor Everywhere

As Franklin took charge, Eleanor tried to find
her own way as first lady. She had mixed feelings about
her new role. Even though she had campaigned hard to
help her husband achieve his lifelong dream, she did not
know what part she could play in his new administration.
"I never wanted to be a president's wife, and don't want
it now," she confessed privately to Lorena Hickok, an
Associated Press reporter, before the inauguration. Yet
at this time of crisis, she said, "We must be able to share
with others whatever may come and . . . meet the future
courageously, with a cheerful spirit."

Immediately Eleanor made it clear that she would be a
different kind of first lady than her predecessors. She did not want
to be waited on—she operated the White House elevator herself,
insisted on driving her own car, and greeted her guests directly. Two
days after the inauguration, she became the first president's wife
to hold regular press conferences—just for female reporters. She
would never trespass on her husband's prerogative by talking
politics, she assured the nation, but she would speak on topics of
interest to women. For Eleanor, these topics included the horrors
of sweatshops and child labor as well as tidbits of traditional female
interest such as White House recipes.

For years, Eleanor had written newspaper and magazine articles.
In 1935, she began a daily syndicated newspaper column called "My
Day," writing about herself and her family, the trips she took, and the
people she met. In addition, during the years that her husband was
president, she gave seventy speeches per year, and wrote nearly five
hundred magazine articles. Like her husband, Eleanor seemed to
possess a reserve of inexhaustible vitality. She seemed to never stop.

While Franklin was running the country from the White
House, Eleanor became his "eyes and ears," traveling around the
country to see things for herself and then report back to her
husband. Over the next few years, Eleanor toured the slums in

Two young men in the
Civilian Conservation
Corps (CCC) doing
forestry work. The
CCC was designed to
tackle the problem of
unemployed young
men between 18 and
25 years old. The
program was based
on the armed forces
model with officers
in charge of workers.
Between 1933 and
1941, 2.5 million men
served in the CCC.

Eleanor accompanies members of the United Mine Workers into an Ohio coal mine in 1935.

Eleanor addressing a conference on negro youth with educator Mary McLeod Bethune by her side.

Washington, D.C., coal mines in West Virginia, **sharecroppers**' farms in the South, and American Indian reservations in the West. People became used to hearing about the adventures of "Eleanor Everywhere" as she toured the highways and byways of the nation. One *New Yorker* magazine cartoon depicted two miners hard at work in a coal mine when one spies a dim figure in the darkness of the mine. "Good gosh," he says. "Here comes Mrs. Roosevelt!"

Through her writing, her speeches, and her travels, the American people began to get to know Eleanor Roosevelt. "I have read and heard so many nice things about you, it's almost like writing to a friend," one admirer wrote her. The woman who had not wanted to be first lady became the nation's most influential advocate for poor and disadvantaged citizens.

One of the groups Eleanor was most concerned about were African Americans. As she traveled the country and witnessed the results of racial prejudice first hand, she became a champion of civil rights. In 1939, she went to Birmingham, Alabama, for the Southern Conference for Human Welfare. She wanted to sit with her friend, African-American educator Mary McLeod Bethune, but was told that it was against the law for a white person to sit on the "colored" side of the auditorium. Eleanor promptly ordered a chair placed in the aisle between the white section and the black section—and sat down.

A few weeks later, the Daughters of the American Revolution (DAR), an organization of women whose ancestors had fought in the American Revolution, refused to let famous African-American singer Marian Anderson give a concert in their hall in Washington, D.C. Eleanor herself was a member of the DAR, and she decided to take a public stand. She resigned and made headlines worldwide. Marian

Anderson ended up giving her concert in front of the Lincoln Memorial, to an audience of more than seventy-five thousand people.

Eleanor was also especially supportive of women's rights. Her 1933 book, *It's Up to the Women*, called on women to enter politics and be at the forefront of the movement for social justice. She urged the president to consider positions for women in government, and he did. Roosevelt was the first president ever to appoint a woman to his cabinet. Frances Perkins became his secretary of labor.

Facing Controversy

Perkins worked with Roosevelt to create the Social Security Act, signed into law on August 14, 1935. By the 1930s, the United States was one of the few Western nations without some sort of pension system for older people. Under the terms of the act, Americans would contribute to a fund that distributed money to elderly, disabled citizens, and those temporarily out of a job. "We can never insure one hundred percent of the population against one hundred percent of the hazards of life," said Roosevelt when he signed the bill, "but we have tried to frame a law which will give some measure of protection to the average citizen and his family against the loss of a job and against poverty-stricken old age."

MORE SECURITY FOR THE AMERICAN FAMILY

WHEN AN INSURED WORKER DIES, LEAVING DEPENDENT CHILDREN AND A WIDOW, BOTH MOTHER AND CHILDREN RECEIVE MONTHLY BENEFITS UNTIL THE LATTER REACH 18.

FOR INFORMATION WRITE OR CALL AT THE NEAREST FIELD OFFICE OF THE **SOCIAL SECURITY BOARD**

A poster advertising the benefits of Social Security.

Not everyone liked Social Security or the other New Deal programs. Conservatives denounced Social Security as a "government giveaway" that would encourage laziness and discourage careful budgeting. They believed that the government should not meddle in the lives of the people. In addition, wealthy people, who disliked Roosevelt because he had raised their taxes, claimed that he was power hungry and "a traitor to his class." Roosevelt insisted, "No one in the United States believes more firmly than I do in the system of private business, private property, and private profit." Yet, he felt that the government had the obligation to actively help people to help themselves.

By 1936, the crisis had passed, but the Depression lingered. Though the New Deal was aiding many people, the economy had still not completely recovered. Nonetheless, to millions of citizens, FDR was a hero, someone who cared about them personally. And when he crossed the country by train to campaign for the 1936 presidential election, they came out in droves to cheer him on.

Roosevelt knew how much some Republicans hated him, but he wasn't daunted. "For twelve years this nation was afflicted with a hear-nothing, see-nothing, do-nothing government," he declared during a campaign speech at Madison Square Garden. "Powerful influences strive today to restore that kind of government. I should like to have it said of my first administration that in it these forces of selfishness and lust for power met their match. I should like to have it said of my second administration that in it these forces met their master."

The people responded, reelecting him by an overwhelming margin of nearly 11 million votes. He won 523 **electoral college** votes out of 531. It was a triumph.

A Second Term

Roosevelt started his second term determined to overcome the major obstacle to his New Deal programs—the Supreme Court. By 1937, the "nine old men," as he called the members of the court, had ruled against eleven of sixteen new laws. They insisted that the legislation gave too much power to the federal government and was unconstitutional. FDR's solution was to try to "pack" the Supreme Court by adding more justices—possibly as many as six—who were favorable to his policies. Republicans as well as many Democrats reacted strongly against the idea. It threatened the separation of powers, they believed, and they refused to support Roosevelt.

President Franklin Roosevelt with Eleanor on the presidential special as they leave Washington, D.C., for a nine-day campaign tour, October 8, 1936.

The attempt to pack the Supreme Court was probably Roosevelt's worst move ever. "He would never have made that mistake," Eleanor said, "if Louis Howe had still been alive." Howe had been with Roosevelt before he was powerful and famous and was not afraid to tell him when he was wrong. Unfortunately, Howe, a chain smoker, had died of a chronic asthma condition in 1936.

Existing New Deal programs were saved when some justices changed their minds and others retired, to be replaced by more liberal judges. In the end, Roosevelt's blunder strengthened his opposition among Republicans and conservative Democrats, and from then on, he had more difficulty getting his laws passed.

Another recession in 1938 caused unemployment to rise again. Not until 1941—and mobilization for World War II—would the workforce finally be fully employed.

At Home in the White House

The White House during the Roosevelt years was a lively place, filled with friends, children, and grandchildren. In addition to Eleanor and Franklin, who each kept a private suite, Louis Howe lived in the family quarters until his death, as did Missy LeHand, Roosevelt's devoted assistant, and Lorena Hickok, the Associated Press reporter who became Eleanor's special friend. After her separation from her first husband, Curtis Dall, daughter Anna moved in with her two children, "Sistie" and "Buzzie," and the other Roosevelt children and their wives lived there from time to time as well. Going to the White House "was like visiting friends in a very large country house," a friend once said.

Every morning, Franklin rose at about 8:00 A.M., read newspapers, and ate breakfast before aides lifted him into his wheelchair for the quick trip down the elevator to the White House office. There, he sat in a swivel chair behind a big desk, read and responded to his mail, pored through government reports, and saw visitors. He spent hours on the telephone—his "legs" and link to the outside world.

Gracious and affable, Roosevelt invariably charmed his guests, even those who differed with him. Behind the charm, however, hid a reserved, even secretive man who kept his true thoughts to himself. When he listened he would smile and nod his head, leading people to believe that he agreed with them. Later, they would be stunned to discover that he didn't. His secretary of the interior, Harold Ickes, once told Roosevelt that he was a very difficult man to work for. "You won't talk frankly with people who are loyal to you," Ickes said to his boss. "You keep your cards close to your belly." Frances Perkins was even more blunt. Roosevelt was the "most complicated human being I ever knew," she said.

At about 5:30 P.M., Roosevelt would go for a swim in the White House pool and perhaps take a short nap. Afterward, during what he called the "children's hour," he would join friends and family in his study for drinks. He spent many evenings playing poker with friends, adding to his enormous stamp collection, or watching movies.

When Eleanor was in Washington, she too kept to a strict schedule. She often started her long day with a horseback ride before breakfast, followed by a packed agenda of meetings, appearances, and press conferences. She always left time to write her daily column and dictate her correspondence to her personal secretary. She and the president led parallel lives, meeting only at certain times during the day. She might dart into his bedroom before breakfast to say hello and come back late at night to talk about issues. Usually they had dinner together, and always, when their children and grandchildren were around, they tried to spend as much time with them as possible.

Franklin and Eleanor pose with the thirteen grandchildren who attended FDR's fourth inauguration, January 20, 1945.

Even Eleanor had difficulty interpreting Roosevelt's poker face. One evening, for instance, he spent a long time arguing with her about a particular policy. The next day he turned around and presented her argument to the ambassador to England. "Without giving me a glance or the satisfaction of batting an eyelash," she remembered later, "he calmly stated as his own the politics and beliefs he had argued against the night before! To this day I have no idea whether he had simply used me as a sounding board, as he so often did . . . or whether my arguments had been needed to fortify his decision and to clarify his mind."

His son James agreed that his father did not open up. "Of what was inside him, of what really drove him, father talked with no one."

Franklin was so busy when his children were growing up that he had not been close to any of his "chicks," as he called them. "When one of my children wanted to see me," he once said, "they had to make an appointment through my secretary. That wasn't the right way." Eleanor, too, often seemed to make time for her children between teaching, writing, making speeches, and traveling. Throughout their lives, the Roosevelt children struggled to make their careers and marriages work. While their parents were in the White House, all five were married and divorced at least once. Everyone agreed that Franklin and Eleanor were much better politicians than parents, yet they loved their children and always made them welcome at the White House, "with their joys and with their sorrows," said Eleanor. "We cannot live other people's lives and we cannot make their decisions for them."

The New Deal

Roosevelt's New Deal offered Americans an "alphabet soup" of recovery programs:

Agricultural Adjustment Administration (AAA): Paid farmers not to grow staple crops to avoid flooding the market with similar produce or goods. Helped diversify farming.

Civilian Conservation Corps (CCC): Hired young men to do construction and conservation work.

Federal Emergency Relief Administration (FERA): Gave aid to state governments for those in need and unemployed citizens.

Federal Deposit Insurance Corporation (FDIC): Insured savings accounts in banks.

National Recovery Administration (NRA): Established regulations and policies for industry such as hours of work, rates of pay, and the fixing of prices.

Rural Electrification Administration (REA): Loaned money to install electricity in rural areas.

Social Security Act (SSA): Distributed pensions to elderly and disabled citizens and unemployment insurance to out of work citizens.

Tennessee Valley Authority (TVA): Built dams to provide electricity in the Tennessee River Valley, built schools, and planted forests.

Works Progress Administration (WPA): Employed teachers, writers, artists, and musicians; put people to work on construction projects.

WORLD WAR

In 1933, the year that Franklin Delano Roosevelt was elected president, a fanatical Austrian named Adolf Hitler was voted into office as the head of the German government. Hitler and his National Socialist German Workers' Party—Nazis— were dedicated to world domination. Within two years after he came to power, Hitler had transformed Germany from a democracy into a **totalitarian** government and had begun an immense military build-up. "Today Germany," he said. "Tomorrow the world!"

Germany was not the only militaristic government to arise in the 1930s. In Italy, **fascist** dictator Benito Mussolini, vowing to build a new Roman Empire, seized Ethiopia in 1935. In Japan, military leaders eager to create a Japanese empire invaded Manchuria and Korea before launching a war against China in 1937.

Adolph Hitler, (left) with Nazi leaders Hermann Goering (center) and Joseph Goebbels (right).

The United States and Europe, weakened by economic depression, sat back and did nothing in the face of this military aggression. The mood in the United States after World War I was strongly isolationist. Protected as they were by two oceans, the United States wanted nothing to do with the problems of Europe and Asia. In 1935, Congress passed a series of Neutrality Acts, signed by Roosevelt, which banned weapons sales or loans to countries at war. During his 1936 reelection campaign, Roosevelt pledged to keep the country out of foreign wars. "I hate war," he declared. "I have passed unnumbered hours . . . thinking and planning how war may be kept from this nation."

Several events, however, caused growing concern. In March of 1938, Hitler invaded and **annexed** Austria. This was followed by other acts of aggression including Germany's seizure of Czechoslovakia's Sudetenland, the territory bordering the northeastern region of Germany. Roosevelt

began to understand the dangers of a do-nothing policy. "I am really worried about world affairs," he wrote a friend. "The dictator nations find their bluffs not being called and that encourages other nations to play the same game."

The War Begins

The crisis came to a head when Germany began a **blitzkrieg,** or lightning war, and crossed the Polish border on September 1, 1939. Two days later, Britain and France declared war on Germany. Still, the United States remained neutral. FDR knew that the American people did not feel threatened enough to take action, even though most were on the side of the Allies, as the anti-Axis nations called themselves.

Roosevelt, realizing the time had come to act, asked Congress to change the Neutrality Acts. Despite opposition from isolationists, a "cash-and-carry" plan was instituted in November 1939, under which the Allied nations could buy arms from the United States as long as they paid in cash and shipped the weapons away in their own vessels.

During those difficult days, Eleanor was especially troubled by the plight of Jewish and other refugees persecuted by Nazis in Europe. Desperate to escape German persecution, they clamored for refuge in the United States. With Franklin's support, she pushed for a measure in Congress that would admit thousands of Jewish children into the country. The nation had strict immigration quotas, however, and neither Congress nor the public wanted to let refugees in. In the end Roosevelt worked behind the scenes to get people **visas** on almost a case-by-case basis. Only a few thousand reached **asylum** in the United States.

World War II

World War II pitted the Allied powers—the United States, Great Britain, France, the Soviet Union, China, and others—against the Axis Powers—Germany, Italy, and Japan. It was fought on three major fronts: Europe, North Africa, and the Pacific. Over a period of six years, 1939–1945, the conflict caused the deaths of approximately sixty million people, soldiers and civilians, around the globe. It was the deadliest and most destructive war in human history.

A Czechoslovakian woman's grief-stricken submission to Nazi invaders in 1939. The war and **occupation** would devastate much of Europe in the next six years.

A Third Term

The big question throughout the early spring of 1940 was whether Roosevelt would run again. If he did and won, he would be the first president ever to serve three terms. Eleanor did not want him to run, and Roosevelt said he would not "unless things get very, very much worse in Europe."

They did. In spring 1940, Germany stormed through Denmark, Norway, Holland, Luxembourg, and Belgium, then pushed into France. On June 14, German troops marched into Paris. By the end of June, only the two small islands of Great Britain lay between Hitler and German domination of the Atlantic Ocean. In a threatening show of mutual support, Germany, Italy, and Japan formed a military alliance called the Berlin-Tokyo-Rome Axis on September 27, 1940.

As Germany attempted to bomb Britain into submission that summer and fall, British prime minister Winston Churchill expressed the defiance of his nation. "We shall defend our island, whatever the cost may be," he declared. "We shall fight on the beaches, we shall fight on the landing grounds, we shall fight in the fields and in the streets, we shall fight in the hills; we shall never surrender." In the United States, the events shocked Congress into allocating money for a massive military build-up and instituting a huge peacetime **draft**.

Roosevelt decided to run again, and Eleanor supported him. At the Democratic National Convention on July 17, Roosevelt was nominated for an unprecedented third term. The delegates were unhappy about his choice of agriculture secretary Henry Wallace for vice president, however, because Wallace used to be a Republican. Perhaps, Franklin suggested, Eleanor could go out to Chicago and speak to the convention on his behalf.

The night of July 18, Eleanor became the first candidate's wife ever to address a national party convention. She reminded the delegates that the person who became president in 1940 faced "a heavier responsibility perhaps, than any man has ever faced before

Eleanor at the Democratic National Convention in Chicago on July 18, 1940.

in this country. . . . You cannot treat it as you would an ordinary nomination in an ordinary time. . . . You will have to rise above considerations which are narrow and partisan. This is a time when it is the United States we fight for." Sobered, the convention calmed down and picked Wallace. Eleanor was widely praised for her speech.

That November, Roosevelt was elected to his third term, by a margin of nearly five million votes. He would be the first—and only—U.S. president to serve three terms in office.

The war was going badly for Great Britain. Winston Churchill, desperate for help, appealed to Roosevelt. "Mr. President, with great respect I must tell you that in the long history of the world this is a thing to do now," he wrote. Roosevelt responded immediately, sending Churchill fifty American destroyers. In spring 1941, when Britain ran out of money to buy military supplies, Roosevelt worked out a program to lend the Allies whatever they needed until they could pay it back.

Roosevelt with his son, Elliot, (right) and Winston Churchill (left) at the Atlantic Conference in August 1941.

In August 1941, Roosevelt sneaked aboard a navy cruiser and sped into the Atlantic Ocean for a top secret meeting with Winston Churchill, the first of nine meetings held during the war. After days of discussion, they signed a document called the Atlantic Charter, which proclaimed that people everywhere had a right to the "four freedoms": freedom of speech, freedom of worship, freedom from want, and freedom from fear. The Charter also called for a "permanent system of general security." A few months later, Roosevelt suggested to Churchill that they call the new organization the "United Nations."

The fall of 1941 was difficult for both Franklin and Eleanor. On September 7, Sara Roosevelt died at age eighty-seven. A few weeks later, Eleanor's brother Hall died from the effects of alcoholism, just as her father had done. Her son James remembered that when Eleanor heard the news, "Father struggled to her side and put his arm around her. 'Sit down,' he said, so tenderly I can still hear it. And he sank down beside her and hugged her and kissed her and held her head on his chest."

"Dr. Win-the-War"

On Sunday, December 7, 1941, Franklin and Eleanor were in the White House together when the news came that the Japanese had bombed the U.S. naval base at Pearl Harbor, Hawaii. In less than two hours, fifteen warships were sunk or damaged and almost two hundred planes destroyed. In her weekly broadcast that afternoon, Eleanor said, "For months now the knowledge that something of this kind might happen has been hanging over our heads. . . . That is all over now and there is no more uncertainty. We know what we have to face and we know that we are ready to face it."

The next day she accompanied the president when he went to Congress. "Yesterday, December 7, 1941—a date which will live in infamy—the United States of America was suddenly and deliberately attacked by naval and air forces of the empire of Japan," Roosevelt said grimly. "No matter how long it may take us to overcome this premeditated invasion, the American people, in their righteous might, will win through to absolute victory." Congress immediately declared war on Japan. Three days later, Germany and Italy declared war on the United States.

Part of the destruction caused by the Japanese sneak attack on Pearl Harbor, Hawaii, December 7, 1941.

Roosevelt threw himself into the war effort. In his words, "Dr. New Deal" became "Dr. Win-the-War." As Japanese forces invaded the Philippines, Burma, Malaya, and the Dutch East Indies and German forces threatened Moscow and Stalingrad, Roosevelt met with Churchill and U.S. and British military officers to create a strategy for the war. He set goals for military production, putting into effect an "arsenal for democracy" that eventually turned out 125,000 planes, 75,000 tanks, and millions of guns per year. On his orders, a nuclear weapon was developed at top secret locations around the country. "I can't tell you what it is, Grace," he told one of his secretaries, "but if it works, and pray God it does, it will save many American lives."

Above all, he inspired and encouraged the nation. "No matter what our enemies . . . in their desperation may attempt to do to us," he said, "we will say as the people of London have said, 'We can take it,' and what is more, we can give it back—with compound interest."

Visiting the War Zone

In 1942, Eleanor Roosevelt accepted an invitation from the British royal family to inspect the war effort in England. After a top-secret flight to London, she took a tour of the bombed-out areas of the city with King George VI and Queen Elizabeth. Over the next two weeks, she attended a state dinner at Buckingham Palace, lunched with female members of Parliament, greeted exiles from other royal houses of Europe, chatted with female British aviators, visited an American bomber squadron, and sat in the cockpit of a Flying Fortress. "I found I'm very fat for the pilot's seat," she joked later.

When she left, a British official reported, "Mrs. Roosevelt has done more to bring a real understanding of the spirit of the United States to the people of Britain than any other single American who has ever visited these islands."

In 1943, she went on a marathon five-week trip to the South Pacific—23,000 miles (about 37,015 kilometers) and seventeen islands in all. Top army officials, convinced she was an ineffectual "do-gooder," had their doubts about her trip. One by one, they were won over, including Admiral William F. "Bull" Halsey, commander of the Pacific Fleet. "I marveled at her hardihood, both physical and mental," he wrote. "She walked for miles, and she saw patients who were grievously and gruesomely wounded. But I marveled most at their expressions as she leaned over them. It was a sight I will never forget."

Eleanor Roosevelt with General Millard Harmon (left) and Admiral William F. Halsey (right) in New Caledonia during her 1943 South Pacific tour.

After visiting camps and hospitals, eating in the mess halls, and seeing about four hundred thousand men, the first lady was proud to report that she left with "a sense of pride in the young people of this generation which I can never express and a sense of obligation which I feel I can never discharge."

Nearing the End

By late 1942, the tide of the war had begun to turn. American and British troops defeated Germany's Afrika Corps in North Africa and then invaded Italy. As the Allies battled their way north on the Italian peninsula, the Soviet army defeated the German forces at Stalingrad and began to push them back through Eastern Europe. In the South Pacific, U.S. troops moved westward from one Japanese-held island to another, taking back the ocean one beach at a time.

Meanwhile, Joseph Stalin, the premier of the Soviet Union, impatiently waited for the Allies to open a second front in Western Europe. In late November 1943, he, Churchill, and Roosevelt met for their first "Big Three" conference in Tehran, Iran, to discuss the coming invasion. The plan was for a massive force to cross the English Channel into France and break the "Atlantic Wall" of concrete forts, minefields, and trenches that the Germans had erected to block the attack. On June 6, 1944—"**D-Day**"—5,300 ships carried the invasion force to France. After a fierce battle, the Allied soldiers slashed through the German defenses and raced toward Paris.

Franklin Roosevelt meeting with Joseph Stalin (left) and Winston Churchill (right) in Teheran, Iran, in 1943.

As the next election neared, Roosevelt began to show signs of exhaustion and ill health. His face was haggard, his body shrunken and wracked by a constant cough. He never considered not running for office, however. He wanted to see the war won and world peace established. Sure enough, he won his fourth term, choosing Missouri congressman Harry S. Truman as his vice president. Then, in late January 1945, he took a long sea voyage to Yalta, a Russian resort town on the Black Sea, for another "Big Three Conference." Churchill was shocked at how ill his friend looked.

Eleanor was also worried about her husband, but that didn't keep her from pressuring him about issues that were important to her—civil rights, labor unions, fair taxes, veterans' benefits, and postwar employment. "I think that sometimes I acted as his conscience," she wrote afterwards. "I urged him to take the harder path when he would have preferred the easier way. In that sense I acted on occasion as a spur, even though the spurring was not always wanted or welcome."

The Final Farewell

After Roosevelt returned from the Yalta conference, he traveled to Warm Springs to relax and regain his strength. The morning of April 12, 1945, he was writing a speech he planned to deliver on Thomas Jefferson's birthday when suddenly he put his hand to his forehead and said, "I have a terrific headache." He fell forward, unconscious. Roosevelt had suffered a massive cerebral hemorrhage. Within three hours, he was dead.

When she heard the news, Eleanor posted a cable to her sons, all but one of whom were fighting overseas: "He did his job to the end as he would want you to do." Then, she flew to Warm Springs and traveled back on the funeral train with the coffin.

Roosevelt's funeral in Hyde Park in 1945.

All along the route, people gathered to pay their respects in the greatest outpouring of grief the country had seen since the death of Abraham Lincoln. Eleanor walked behind the coffin as it was carried into the White House for a memorial service. On Sunday, April 15, 1945, she saw her husband buried in his mother's rose garden at Hyde Park.

A few days later, a reporter stopped Eleanor outside her New York City apartment and asked her for a statement. "The story is over," Eleanor said simply. She was wrong.

CHAPTER SEVEN

FIRST LADY OF THE WORLD

When Franklin died, Eleanor Roosevelt was only sixty years old, still healthy and energetic. "I did not want to cease trying to be useful in some way," she said. Yet what role could she play in the postwar world?

From Hyde Park she watched the last act of the war unfold—the surrender of Germany on May 7, 1945, and the surrender of Japan on August 14. The new president, Harry S. Truman, treasured Eleanor's advice, and she did what she could to aid him in the first days of the new administration. He asked her to be one of five delegates to the new United Nations (UN) Assembly held in London in December 1945. She accepted, with some trepidation, grateful for a chance to further what she felt was her husband's most lasting contribution to world peace.

Her fellow U.S. delegates, a group of all male senators and other government officials, did not expect much from her because she was a woman. They assigned her to Committee Three, on humanitarian, educational, and cultural questions, thinking that it would be less important than the political and economic committees. Yet one of the most important issues ended up in her committee—the issue of what to do with the nearly one million displaced people in refugee camps throughout Europe. These were people who had been imprisoned in concentration or work camps or who had been made homeless during the war. The Russians wanted them to be forced to return to their countries of origin. The United States felt the refugees should choose their own homeland. Eleanor Roosevelt had to argue her case against Andrei Vishinsky, the Soviet Union's top speaker in the General Assembly. The delegates voted—and upheld the position of the United States. Mrs. Roosevelt was one of the most vital members of the committee, her fellow delegates concluded.

As a UN delegate for seven years, Eleanor tried to build "real goodwill for people throughout the world" and enlarge and increase the humanitarian work of the organization. In 1946, she was appointed chairman of the United Nations Commission on Human Rights, which was charged with drafting an international bill of rights. She drove her committee members for twelve- and fourteen-hour days until they came up with a document acceptable to all. Eleanor insisted that the declaration be written in plain language, so that everyone around the world could understand it. When it was approved on December 10, 1948, the General Assembly rose and gave her a standing ovation.

Goodwill Ambassador

Eleanor's time at the UN ended with the 1952 election of Republican president Dwight D. Eisenhower, who did not reappoint her. Before, she had been an official goodwill ambassador of the United States to the world. Now, she became an unofficial ambassador, traveling to India, Japan, Israel, Indonesia, Europe, Turkey, and many other countries. In 1957, she finally had the opportunity to visit the Soviet Union, about which she had been curious for a long time. At Nikita Khrushchev's summer villa in Yalta, she had a long conversation with the new Soviet premier about the arms race and the **Cold War.** When she was leaving, Khrushchev asked her, "Can I tell our papers that we have had a friendly conversation?"

"You can say that we had a friendly conversation but that we differ," she replied.

Despite their differences, she invited him to Hyde Park for tea when he came to the United States. When she was criticized by the press for entertaining a communist leader, she answered, "We have to face the fact that either all of us are going to die together or we are going to learn to live together and if we are to live together, we have to talk."

Eleanor Roosevelt (center) and Nina (left) and Nikita (right) Khrushchev at the Franklin D. Roosevelt Library in Hyde Park in September 1959.

Eleanor Roosevelt, Human Rights Advocate

In 1958, Eleanor delivered an address to the United Nations General Assembly on human rights:

"Where, after all, do universal human rights begin? In small places, close to home—so close and so small that they cannot be seen on any maps of the world. Yet they are the world of the individual persons; the neighborhood he lives in; the school or college he attends; the factory, farm, or office where he works. Such are the places where every man, woman, and child seeks equal justice, equal opportunity, equal dignity without discrimination. Unless these rights have meaning there, they have little meaning anywhere. Without concerned citizen action to uphold them close to home, we shall look in vain for progress in the larger world."

There was a steady stream of world leaders, as well as friends and family, to Val-Kill, the cottage that Eleanor made her home for the last seventeen years of her life. Sons Elliot and John and their families also had homes on the property, and her nineteen grandchildren and four great-grandchildren visited regularly, to swim in the pool and have picnics on the grounds. "I treasure the love of my children," she said at a celebration for her seventieth birthday, "the respect of my children, and I would never want my children or my grandchildren to feel that I had failed them."

She continued her other activities, too, still writing her "My Day" column, hosting a television talk show, and teaching at Brandeis University in Massachusetts. When Democrat John F. Kennedy became president in 1960, he appointed her as a delegate to the United Nations once more. Year after year, opinion polls named her the most admired woman in the world. She knew that someday she would have to slow down, but in the meantime, she declared, "Life has got to be lived—that's all there is to it."

She was finally forced to slacken her pace when she was diagnosed with aplastic anemia, a rare blood disease, in the early 1960s. On November 7, 1962, Eleanor Roosevelt died in her town house in New York City. A few days later, she was laid to rest in the rose garden at Hyde Park, next to her husband. President Kennedy, past presidents Harry S. Truman and Dwight Eisenhower, and future president Lyndon Johnson all attended the funeral of the extraordinary woman Truman called the First Lady of the World.

President John F. Kennedy, former President Harry S. Truman, Vice President Lyndon B. Johnson, and former President Dwight D. Eisenhower at Eleanor Roosevelt's funeral in Hyde Park in 1962.

1882	Franklin Delano Roosevelt is born on January 30
1884	Anna Eleanor Roosevelt is born on October 11
1899	Eleanor attends Allenswood School
1900	Franklin attends Harvard
1903	Franklin graduates from Harvard; Franklin and Eleanor become engaged
1905	Franklin and Eleanor marry on March 17
1906	Anna Roosevelt is born on May 6
1907	James Roosevelt is born on December 23
1909	Franklin Jr. is born on March 18 and dies of influenza
1910	Franklin is elected to the New York State Senate; Elliot is born on September 23
1913	Franklin is appointed assistant secretary of the Navy
1914	The second Franklin Jr. is born on August 17; World War I begins on August 1
1916	John is born on March 17
1918	World War I ends on November 11
1920	Franklin runs for vice president
1921	Franklin is stricken with polio
1922	Eleanor joins Women's Trade Union League and Democratic State Committee
1928	Franklin is elected governor of New York
1929	Great Depression begins
1932	Franklin is elected president on November 8
1933	Franklin is inaugurated on March 4; in first Hundred Days, Franklin creates the New Deal
1935	Franklin signs Social Security Act on August 14
1936	Franklin is elected president for a second term on November 3
1939	Germany invades Poland on September 1 and World War II begins; "cash and carry" program is passed by Congress on November 4
1940	Franklin is elected president for a third term on November 5; lend-lease program and peacetime draft begin
1941	Japanese bomb Pearl Harbor on December 7; United States declares war against Japan; Germany and Italy declare war against the United States
1942	Eleanor Roosevelt visits England upon invitation from the British royal family
1943	Eleanor travels to South Pacific to see U.S. troops; Franklin meets with Joseph Stalin and Winston Churchill in Tehran on November 28
1944	Allied forces land in France on June 6; Franklin is reelected president for a fourth term on November 7
1945	Franklin meets with Churchill and Stalin again in Yalta on February 4; Franklin dies on April 12; on May 7, Germany surrenders; on August 14, Japan surrenders; Eleanor serves as U.S. delegate to the United Nations (UN)
1946	Eleanor heads committee that drafts Declaration of Human Rights
1952	Eleanor resigns from the UN
1957	Eleanor visits the Soviet Union and meets Nikita Khrushchev
1961	President Kennedy reappoints Eleanor to the UN
1962	Eleanor dies on November 7

activism—trying to make social or political change through active involvement.

annex—to take over territory (usually by force) and merge it with an existing nation or city.

asylum—protection given by one country to citizens of another country who are seeking to avoid cruel treatment or poor conditions in their homeland.

blitzkrieg—(German word meaning "lightning war") A military strategy designed to shock enemy forces through the use of surprise, speed, and weaponry. Tested by the Germans during the Spanish Civil War in 1938 and against Poland in 1939, the blitzkrieg proved to be a terrifying combination of land and air attacks.

Cold War—state of political tension and military rivalry that existed between the United States and the Soviet Union following World War II.

D-Day—literally translates to "Day-Day." Originally the code name for the day on which a military offensive is to be launched. Specifically refers to June 6, 1944, the Allied invasion of Normandy, France.

diphtheria—bacterial disease that creates a thick coating in the nose, throat, or airway. This coating can cause breathing problems, heart failure, paralysis, and sometimes death.

draft—to select one or more people for participation in forced military service.

electoral college—group of electors from each state that votes for the president and vice president of the United States, based on the popular vote in each state.

fascist—person who belongs to or supports a system of government characterized by strong, often absolute control over political and economic affairs.

isolationist—person who believes in a policy of noninvolvement with other nations.

laissez-faire—(French expression meaning "let alone") The belief that government should play a minimal role in business affairs.

monopoly—complete control over a service or product within a given area; a company that exerts such control.

national convention—meeting held by the two major national political parties to select party candidates for the upcoming presidential elections.

occupation—the invasion and control of a country or territory by enemy forces.

sharecropper—farmer who rents land and gives a portion of his or her crop to the owner of the land as payment.

Spanish-American War (1898)—conflict between the United States and Spain that ended Spanish colonial rule in the New World.

suffrage—the right to vote.

sweatshop—business employing laborers at low wages, for unreasonable hours, or under unhealthy conditions.

Tammany Hall—New York Democratic Party organization, founded in 1789, historically exercising corrupt political control. The name comes from a pre-Revolutionary association named after Tammanend, a Delaware Native American chief.

tenement—city apartment in a six- or seven-floor building, usually possessing limited facilities such as little sunlight and poor sanitary conditions.

totalitarian—describes a one-party system of government that exerts absolute control over the lives of its citizens.

typhoid fever—bacterial disease that is characterized by high fever, diarrhea, and swelling of the intestines and is spread through infected food or water.

visa—official document allowing its bearer to enter and travel within a foreign nation.

FURTHER INFORMATION

Further Reading

Ambrose, Stephen E. *The Good Fight: How World War II Was Won.* New York: Atheneum, 2001.

Brown, Jonatha A. *Eleanor Roosevelt.* (Trailblazers of the Modern World). Milwaukee: World Almanac Library, 2002.

Doak, Robin. *Franklin D. Roosevelt.* (Trailblazers of the Modern World). Milwaukee: World Almanac Library, 2002.

Downing, David. *The Great Depression.* (20th Century Perspectives). Chicago: Heinemann Library, 2001.

Freedman, Russell. *Eleanor Roosevelt: A Life of Discovery.* Boston: Houghton Mifflin, 1997.

Gormley, Beatrice. *First Ladies: Women Who Called the White House Home.* Madison, WI: Turtleback Books, 2004.

Horn, Geoffrey M. *Theodore Roosevelt.* (Trailblazers of the Modern World). Milwaukee: World Almanac Library, 2004.

Kraft, Betsey Harvey. *Theodore Roosevelt: Champion of the American Spirit.* Boston: Clarion Books, 2003.

Krull, Kathleen. *V is for Victory: America Remembers World War II.* (American History Classics). New York: Knopf, 2002.

Kudlinski, Kathleen. *Franklin Delano Roosevelt: Champion of Freedom.* (Childhood of Famous Americans). New York: Aladdin, 2003.

MacGowen, Tom. *The Attack on Pearl Harbor.* (Cornerstones of Freedom). Danbury, CT: Children's Press, 2002.

Mara, Wil. *Franklin D. Roosevelt.* (Rookie Biographies). Danbury, CT: Children's Press, 2004.

Mayo, Edith P. (ed). *The Smithsonian Book of First Ladies: Their Lives, Times and Issues.* New York: Henry Holt/Smithsonian Institution, 1996.

Schuman, Michael A. *Franklin D. Roosevelt: The Four-Term President.* (People to Know). Berkeley Heights, NJ: Enslow, 1996.

Wroble, Lisa A. *The New Deal and the Great Depression in American History.* (In American History). Berkeley Heights, NJ: Enslow, 2002.

FURTHER INFORMATION

Places to Visit

Franklin D. Roosevelt Presidential
  Library and Museum
  4079 Albany Post Road
  Hyde Park, NY 12538
  (845) 486-7770

Sagamore Hill (Home of
  Theodore Roosevelt)
  20 Sagamore Hill Road
  Oyster Bay, NY 11771-1809
  (516) 922-4788

Smithsonian National Museum of
  American History
  14th Street and Constitution
    Avenue N.W.
  Washington, D.C. 20560
  (202) 633-1000

The Eleanor Roosevelt Center
  at Val-Kill Stone Cottage
  56 Val-Kill Road
  Hyde Park, NY 12538
  (845) 229-5302

The National First Ladies' Library
  Education and Research Center
  205 Market Avenue South
  Canton, Ohio 44702
  (330) 452-0876

Theodore Roosevelt Birthplace
  National Historic Site
  28 East 20th Street
  New York, NY 10003
  (212) 260-1616

White House
  1600 Pennsylvania Avenue, N.W.
  Washington, D.C. 20500
  (202) 456-2121

Web Sites

The National First Ladies' Library
www.firstladies.org

Roosevelt's home at Hyde Park
www.nps.gov/hofr/

Roosevelt library
www.fdrlibrary.marist.edu/index.html

Sagamore Hill
www.nps.gov/sahi/

Theodore and Elliot Roosevelt's birthplace
in New York City
www.nps.gov/thrb/

The White House
www.whitehouse.gov

Page numbers in **bold** represent photographs.

About the Author

Ruth Ashby has written many award-winning biographies and
nonfiction books for children, including *Herstory*, *The Elizabethan
Age*, and *Pteranodon: The Life Story of a Pterosaur*. She lives on Long
Island with her husband, daughter, and dog, Nubby.

www.ingramcontent.com/pod-product-compliance
Lightning Source LLC
Chambersburg PA
CBHW060801150426

42813CB00058B/2802